THE BODYFEEL LEXICON

Jessica Bozek

SWITCHBACK BOOKS

CHICAGO

ALSO BY JESSICA BOZEK

cor·re·spond·ence, with Eli Queen
(dusi/e-chap kollektiv, 2007)

ISBN-13: 978-0-9786172-4-0

ISBN-10: 0-9786172-4-X

LIBRARY OF CONGRESS CONTROL NUMBER: 2008941726

Book design: Eli Queen

Cover art: Joseph Beuys

TELEPHONE T--R [UPSIDE DOWN R], 1974

Two tin cans, twine, label, brown paint; 11.8 x 20.2 x 10.1 cm (4 5/8 x 7 15/16 x 4 in.)

Harvard University Art Museums, Busch-Reisinger Museum, The Willy and Charlotte Reber

Collection, Louise Haskell Daly Fund, 1995.315

Photo: Junius Beebe © President and Fellows of Harvard College

Switchback Books

Brandi Homan, *Editor-in-Chief*

Becca Klaver and Hanna Andrews, *Founding Editors*

Melissa Severin, *Managing Editor*

PO Box 478868

Chicago, IL 60647

editors@switchbackbooks.com

www.switchbackbooks.com

for Eli

TABLE OF CONTENTS

The Transports

An Airborne Torpor

The Sequence Between Molars

The Matchbook Fragments

Appendices

THE PEARY ASSEMBLAGE: ON THE REMNANT CORRESPONDENCE AND EPHEMERA OF AN UNIDENTIFIED WOLF AND LEON SZKLAR

Three years ago, I traveled to the North American tundra to study the curious social behavior of the arctic wolf. I was able to observe and interact with various packs above the Arctic Circle (see *Bulletin of the Canadian Zoological Society*, Winter 2005). One day, while exploring a former wolf den in a rocky outcropping, I discovered a singular parcel. Wrapped in the skin of a Peary caribou I found a collection of letters and other documents. Because such skin, once separated from a caribou's carcass, ceases to give off any scent, the parcel had likely remained undisturbed by foraging animals. No doubt, the tundra's extreme temperatures also aided in the preservation of the documents. Reproductions of these documents, now known collectively as The Peary Assemblage, follow.

Regarding the origins of The Peary Assemblage, it has been determined that there were two interlocutors: a pair of lovers named Wolf and Leon Szklar. Establishing Wolf's identity with any certainty, however, has proved an impossible task. She is seldom referred to by another name, and not once is even the most diligent reader rewarded with a clue as to what her first name might have been. Excepting the existence of The Peary Assemblage, Wolf's disappearance from the world appears total.

In Szklar's case, it was possible to check the photography credits in various wildlife publications from the previous decade and then link the "L. Szklar" beside many sub-Saharan images with the "L," "Leo," "Leon," and "Leopard" of the letters in the Wolf-Szklar correspondence. A brief notice in the May 2000 issue of *International Wildlife* attributes Szklar's "attraction to outmoded technologies and to the bird's-eye view" as crucial factors in his death when the hot-air balloon he was traveling in crashed on the Yukon Plateau.

The order of the documents within The Peary Assemblage remains unaltered here. I found each section bound and titled. It will likely be clear to readers from the subject matter that Wolf authored the pieces in *An Airborne Torpor* and Szklar those in *The Transports*. Still, there is some question about the authorship of The Peary Assemblage's other documents. *The Matchbook Fragments* were indeed configured on hundreds of matchbooks. Each "exhibit" presents the contents of individual plastic bags labeled "1a," "1b," etc. It is possible that Wolf, in imitation of ungulate predation, composed both series to suggest that correspondence is a compensatory act (i.e., what dies—the worlds that slip away—would have died all the same). However, if that possibility were ruled out, it would still be uncertain which of our authors was responsible for the "a" series and which for the "b" series.

Finally, except where authorship is obvious, the assemblage's appendices are perhaps best approached as Wolf and Szklar's attempt at the creation of a collaborative mythology.

—*The Editor*

THE CALENDAR WAS THE SAFEST THING
THEY EVER READ

In the theater of strapless extremity, they averted the tourists' eyes. Not to the heavy curtains undrawn, their missing flutter-labor, but for the entrance the tourists gasped. The performers warbled a way to bird, raised bird to wolf, framed wolf for leopard, posed leopard for wolf. How would they take it all back?

Drawers pulled out, slipped back in, other after another. One Ms. Wolf, two Mr. Szklar: glassy game-players from the journals they pretended to keep for themselves but left behind in a gouge of subway cars & folded into coat pockets evenings at the opera's clothes-keep. Pimpek, their mutt, rumbled low over wide stone windowsills when the tenor began.

They slunk into the nether birdhouse & grew new animals to replace the dog, who had besides grown his own epistolary impulse. They promised to send stamps, to seek out fictile surfaces for their correspondence. Inside a birdhouse-for-big-birds they secreted the shuttering embraces, alarm-eyes & winnowed paint chips. Their collection of wheels they split by century. One set, from a kaiserin's carriage, they sent to auction. He wrapped her wrap in tissue paper. She traded his teeth for hunting savvy. Plots in hand, they spent a last day in human quiet, wind a soft-pedaled animality.

Goodbye toothpaste & damage-sift. Goodbye calendrical urges. Goodbye they waved & wavered. Goodbye one peeked, goodbye the other pulled her umbrella closer.

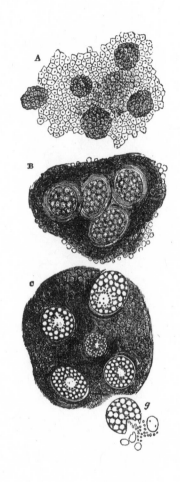

A HOT-AIR BALLOON
IS QUIETER, SLOWER

Dear dear,

All photography is: striking. Another way, I wind out a stepped authenticity. I snap the animals stunned. Now they are shot and the negatives fixed. New twine lines up to hover the figures in tall grasses. My pulse keeps pace with the candle's shadow upon the ocelot-skin walls.

When the waters rise, I'll leave. The highest part of the sun will be at my head, read in someone else's camera. No wisdom hoots in hell.

Revise my geography.

Yours,
Leon

Dear L,

I'm at the side of splitting my invisible seams. The visible ones
too—baby fat stripes above & below elbows, across stomach & hips.
My parents tripped often & I took steps in my crib pretending myself
halfway across the world—until I settled my textbook-correct heft on
a pillow, canary-yellow, sewn up from an old cashmere sweater.

The pillow I remember better, though, was my first on a bed. Full-
sized, brown on one side, fierce Lion on the other. They insisted on a
case, on insult—a lack of respect for habitat. When the cage persisted,
I maintained the dormant mouth close to open.

A bag lady lived in the space between the wall & my bed. Her bags
& cats & mangy fur coat could not have fit, let alone she, though
removed & thin. Yet I dwelled on her & made a pact with Lion. If
ever she tried to crawl up from that narrow space, then he would raise
his head from the pillow, lift it high through the opening & roar. He
came to all the hotels, camp cabins, school.

Lion was my first.

Why Leopard, yours.

Dear Wolf,

Take me into the songs whose lyrics promise convertible rides toward sunset and declarations of eternal love as mile-markers descend.

My mother tried to go there, smiling a little too hopefully at the bored men on vinyl stools. She let us dip french fries in ranch dressing. Deprived of our need to need, we fidgeted less, were interested. She flew a helicopter on her back. It was important that the landing gear never touch the ground—in this case, linoleum in unpalatable shades of brown.

At home we listened along doorjambs, the beadboard was splitting apart, and the swing-set our dream house.

The soap smelled of almond extract, though we didn't yet know it.

But there she was. Already beginning to leave.

Leo

Oh, Leo!

Instead of photographs you should offer the world an accordion-
book model of the self: each new page a stacked evasion of the last. A
wreck at the end, that attempt to fix a mother in memory as animals
in a camera. Exercises in montage, a popsicle stick-yielding zoetrope.
Revolve the model between palms to dizzy away your predatory stand-
ins for place.

While I've decided on remotest northwest, a smothering hold. The
alpha's bestowal of past pup skin or fresh kill to mismatch my hide.
You'll be farther still, further restless, but so intent on revision, were
you ever coming back? The dripping mouthpiece what wind dropped,
speech reducing to taillights in a lapidary hush. I never questioned
your existence.

By turns festive, grieving. By turns the left lover, the right woman for
a scandal. I'm trained at carrying my capital self in felicitous coats.
No longer prey to the disguises & manipulations of this husk, I'll try
extreme better than you.

Wolf

Dear Applicant,

In your studies of bodyfeel, have you found an equation to measure the rate at which flush seeps from skin? And how does one say "scars that do not make good stories" in the bodyfeel lexicon? Current theory holds that as a body hardens, its imprecisions lessen.

When did you decide you didn't like your given? Was it adolescent sports, the lore of last name on your jersey back? A distance from diminutive, a way to animal, and an excuse for the monster noises viscous food on your tongue provoked. The troll-under-everything my favorite, your best.

You never let me call you by your first name.

Cordially,
Leon Szklar

Let's pretend, Leo, that animals need not become human interest stories, that wolf need not be *den mother*, *maternal instinct*; & leopard *spots for sexy underwear*, *safari-themed stocking stuffer*.

We'll hide our secrets under animal fat & felt, send friends telegrams that wink, "I am still alive." We'll stand intent on revision, then tumble the blocks.

We could not have been less known. To movie you—vaguely *and* specifically enough: exact amounts of each render transformation for the other.

Whole is no assertion. Divide with me.

Yours.

Dear Wolf,

Far enough now to be vitric remembrance, another figure to ignore up on a ledge. Would you have me pressed, carnival, or etched? Hobnail or crown?

What a life's work—to find and love the live ones, all so named and finished—your alabaster eagle, corrugated caterpillar, roiled sea snake. The dioramas obscured.

Dusty, did I become a stretch?

Less pervious,
glassy, glacier, glaze

Dear Leo,

Scent marks, a greater range of vocalizations—these will be new. How right to be at the top of a food chain, to have 42 teeth (instead of the six I was born to lack), to live in harmony with a group.

In the winter my tail will keep me warm. Ingenious, the rounding up of self, the animal coiling. Moving a head into it, sometimes slowly, sometimes greedily. I sneeze & wait for the moment I'll lose my human frame of reference. When memory will be scent & seasonal, when movement will be fast & fur-hard.

But I'm scared to lose.

What do studies say about the lupine subconscious? What can they say about ours? We can't tap a hole in the side of a head, stick a milkshake straw in, & simply film.

What if I went to, at first, a circle of drive-in screens & then a walking into & out of worlds? Not the tundra, not instinctual,

Wolf

My fur ruse,

To prevent my running away in daydreams, I needed to be tied up. My idea. I liked to struggle against the dirty rope. I liked to get free. I should have recognized that life would always be topography built up to be leveled. The reconstructions were similar. Sometimes a ceiling fan stood in for an air conditioner, but my poorly shaven Adam's apple remained. My strong fingernails tore still at the binds. My fading shoulder freckles kept right on fading.

When my spots come in, come to me.

Your whelp

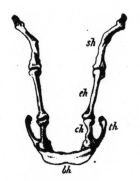

THE MATCHBOOK FRAGMENTS

OPENING EXHIB.

it's the usual diss
-olution
of cymophanous swelling

on toast: the
double-head Harlequin
slow of it

signal to cloud
into a swoon
blotting
our still

the wide-eyed tourist
sleep & quiet
transience of it
seemly

EXHIB. 1A

my retroflex you

wherefore punctate
I gulped
a shot past
the steppy space

post like vowels
every fourth to eighth
letter/day
broke something on my head

a wide weight sack-like
slowing me into this

dear leo

EXHIB. 1B

day eight

dear head
the vowels past you
post me retroflex into this

like/like

I broke wide
the fourth weight
every punctate space-
sack shot

wherefore some gulped

EXHIB. 2A

I sat up with it
skimmed the glass-top
echoing bubbles

not before
to pass fracture
with valises all

in another tongue I don't know
in this (one) grow goodbye

to sluggish brittle & forget

EXHIB. 2B

good with sluggish

tongue-fracture echo
skimmed another I
grow (glass) before
forget-bubbles

brittle up
& know this
with bye

any language?
the friend of certificates
passages & prom-hair

I'm getting away
because I do

some animals will be harmed
in the production of this

it may not break your heart
to learn it

is a swelling

EXHIB. 3B

because I'm swelling
to break your language

prom-learn
harmed certificate
hair-prod

is any friend
getting animals
a way/heart
past this?

some passages do

EXHIB. 4A

dear un-
less real
unless I

I've never held a gun
in my anodyne seams

where I am wax
walls extend
up from
the roof inside

arsenal raindrops
are bullets

to-do lists erase
themselves & ghosts
don't float this
architecture I prefer
to most

EXHIB. 4B

I've never held architecture
unless ghosts
dear-less
themselves are arsenal

I prefer the roof
a gun to most walls

wax seams
rain anodyne
float lists

to-do bullets
extend from erase

EXHIB. 5A

our pecan love
is past if
you'd returned
dear l

I might have smelled you
out of act-
ion I compacted
the contents of my a
-ccounts to say   .

you sheared by
more than charge

EXHIB. 5B

say
if you smell
my compacted love
the sheared
might of dear

return a-charge
act more out of you

THE TRANSPORTS

wherein "I leave you" means "I shear you,
I give up my share"

THE LEOPARD'S PRAYER

Sick rattle below. Fermenting snore along. I fixated not on feudal maiden rape, as did the social studies teacher, who wanted one girl, mousse-crunched, on the back of a motorcycle he didn't have. Knightly.

Our touching was hands once. Her father and I wore sweatshirts from the same wildlife preservation series. His was the lesser panda. Mine was too big, a man's, over a sweater. I kissed her in my head. I kissed her on the mouth. Ungracefully but long. Eyes glutted shut with embarrassment, I bore down so that she couldn't protest.

Electrical systems. A breadbox kept me whole and clammy: rumpy waiting to enter my adolescent frame.

Reared in bars, I sunk pool balls like stingers.

Debbie (neighborhood transvestite, partial to spandex)—my vote for mom's new best friend.

Letting him in finally. And real licks.

I was concerned with repetition and cavern, the failure to tally right as a rupture above the next day.

Toe-lint constellations on the walls were a shrine. I gave up my body in ever-renewing bits.

THE CARCASS TRANSPORT

My camera makes   : a must of us
                    : "for posterity's sake" your posterior skin

You might wonder how a man who has forsaken helicopters takes
his agitation. And he would tell you, resoundingly, exclamation
points—another version of trying to fell sleep.

Let's go the other—aperture a letter, animate a script.

"Mayakovsky's house brain"   I want to make a muss of you!

But mold-clots, the two-dimensional captures.

THE STATIONER'S TRANSPORT

through panes and across sheets, perception yields

here, in the margins, my body-ghosts happen

though filaments are slippery, hems stay threaded in the wind

on the savanna no new-season snow

I repeat your name and follow horizontals

distracted hands make sludge of a self

as rough rounds corkscrew the sky

the grounds of my love—sweat-peel, tragus-ring smatter, cuticalia—

air-lit by the replica moons of a three-hole punch

THE GEOMETRY TRANSPORT

Training for a transport
of turns and time-skew

should include pre-notes,
practiced angles. Traveling

songs to bloom correspond-
dence: I sine you, you

circumscribe me. Let
the tools of our Hyphen War

be: quadruped-smell,
hand-breath. Long on

the ground, late at
the gorge. Tooth-lit.

Leanings aren't weight-
loss biscuits, nor tendencies;

they are vulnerabilities.
I left leaning

against your half-
walls—something

to remember me down.
Geometry stutters, un-

leads its mechanical pencils,
stubs to eraser-casing.

Who slopes along
inscribes a slant for sniff.

THE LEAF TRANSPORT

My fall leavings were hand-swept—a seeding. You, my tree, what leaves on the ground. Brittled to a pulp.

"Leo, leaf me," you pressed. The old leaves-die-leafs-light. You're left all the same. A boring to bear.

Where you, kempt to the frame, kept figurines and postcards for their proximity to experience, I snuck portions of you, now finger the offs and outs, cast thefts across my chest in a bitty embrace.

To close, you loathed me too close. Leave me seasoned in what's left: your tissued cloud and linten vole.

Love a leaf feller

NOTES FOR ANOTHER GEOMETRY TRANSPORT

1. Bridges of view. Girded by the accumulation of our unremitting
   swerves, eyes arc to follow a fault I could melt into.

2. Ice, must and mutating letters—a peristalsis of flash cubes.
   Lust evades like a common latitude. A list in the margins,
   running accusatory. To swap is not to understand, is not
   to know the storms and stories, the trees and tents.

3. Rehearse my floating body. When you come, snow-wet,
   my anti-bride.

THE LEOPARD TRANSPORT

The leopard transport serves tea and cassava leaf-wrapped wildebeest tail to VIPs only. A leopard like me settles for the irregulars, the non-native cast-offs of the human transports. Leopards read the financial times, the flood times, the forest fire times, the topical times. Leopards thrive without passports and prefer to travel by foot. The climate-controlled air of the transport twitches us.

A leopard alone in the transport is a leper. Leo, a proto-leopard. The leopard transport is the rest of rest.

I parse and pick. How our sex was rutted: you were too total for *as*. My aesthetic was more Schiele splotches of strawberry red across nipples, gnarled green knuckles brushing simple black lines.

And now, you have the sky, the distant hole of it. Every night a new swath. But are you never partial to certain configurations of stars?

Transport cannot answer our evolutions, our lootings of ourselves and the animals in picture books, reference manuals, and zoological studies. The animals themselves. Transport is but voluble pupae.

In our separate roams. On our two flats. The dried green and the blinding white. The sweat shattering, teeth chattering. The bone lengthening, nose broadening.

Tell me if you are still you—not physically. Voraciously.

THE TRANSPORT BOUND

In a ghost   fire limbs, a grave
projection: you here, who wouldn't

                pinion   if I implored you.
                I spent the day watching

                Who   me stiffs me
                in still minutes. Slower I don't think of you.

The   I stage, the release I resist.
For its insomnia and fallow turns.

                We lie low,   yet when we speak.
                I keep such a greyed cord.

Ask for your   to fasten me
but twice a year. This ring around myself

        play another way.
I'm out here, bound

                to be a matter   or credit.
                If you don't miss me tonight, pull

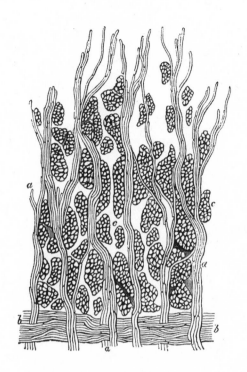

AN AIRBORNE TORPOR

[BOEING 757]

An inch from the lavatory mirror, my eyes burn with finger-residue
trapped under lenses. I'm not doubled, but fattened, fuzzed—like a
bloated aunt. Someone I've looked at always & admired—until the
day I saw her in myself. It might be vanity (that nose looks fine on her,
but not on me). I've never had a problem classifying others—*looks
right in scrubs, overweight & a better dancer for it*, etc.

My pretense more a post-tense: I presume I will be (happier, furrier),
I presume this will work. So the sympathy card supposes we go to a
better place when we die.

If I thought we'd find a consistency, not spare or botulized, but
tapioca pearl-firm, I'd find a plane to you, pet your spots, catch leaves
with you under unused trestles. If you have them there.

[BOEING MD-80]

Steel wool sky—scrubbed dull, scrubbed same. A window-bound version of the vast & squint-essential tundra for mapping wolf.

Everything is not my way of getting back at you.

I crossed: my name off a threshold, a street, an x-ray machine, a spurt of water, this flight off a mountain range, a palette of international diaper waste smeared across the desert, a border, my legs. (Your mind?)

Talk. Breed. Hatch. Fade.

Hurry, horizons are a myth. A meth-dream. Anagrammed, our names pedal or flow.

I flow if low. See wolf everywhere. See star-bomb, see abrasive spores.

Please, miss, bring me a blanket for conjuring claws & the pups' fast clinging licks, as if they could shape me into a wolf with their tongues.

[CESSNA 206]

Dear photographer, don't forget to crop me out.

Freightless, I waivered. The pilot ascented.

As fog systems collide, 1a, a pert bob, picks at her cuticles. The strip already superficial, but tethered still. Lined up on her armrest, dead & dying all the time.

2a nibbles from the saltine sleeve & unwrapped pickle in her jacket pockets, is going the long way to Mongolia for Ulaanbaatar's living payphones, the masked women with white desk phones.

If you saw 2a from afar, you might mistake her for an adolescent. But for the corner crinkling of her eyes.

Compelled to disclosure, 2a recounts a Greyhound ride one month earlier to visit her Russian entomologist. After ten hours she was the only passenger on the bus & the driver needed a break. He offered her a backrub, promising to make up the time when they were on the road again. He pulled off at a no-name motel. He opened the door, did not turn on the air conditioning unit. She removed her cardigan & sat cross-legged in the center of the bed. They were on the bus again in 35 minutes.

Double scotch. All the rocks. Listen. A landing. I bore fingernails into the vinyl seat, mouth lupine vocalizations into the throttled air.

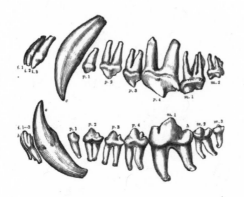

THE SEQUENCE BETWEEN MOLARS

Dear Tented Leopard,

In a zoology I am taken on the plow. Picture my succumbing to the bulk & red & whisky-warm breath of restless men, clearing licked-fur snowfields.

But that is not the way to wolf. In the days before the pups knew to select the shortest route in their pursuit, I was their play prey. By age two months they could attack from all corners in high, curved jumps. Now accurate in seizing me, one grasped my neck, another my side, the third my rear, the fourth my leg, & the last placed her paws on my back, pushing me to the ground. The killing bite. & when blood appeared, the bite-&-shake.

Once, I tripped over your name, afraid to lose it. Once, I imagined your smell as the space between—winter & wild, snow & grass. I have come home to range. One letter shy of a drift.

wolf

Dear Supplicant,

Confined for a night, how will I dream devastated in so many languages?

Gas-pumps add alarm-air to the tires of your long dark plow—a quarter an hour cushions it from theft.

Yours,
Leopard

Leopard,

I close my eyes, rounder now, & the world appears rubbed out along its circumference—a black eraser to my fact. Woozy as in the assisted sleeps I craved, only it's the hardest cold, so hard it makes me soft, so soft I can't stay awake. But I want to be so alert I can't remember your leavings—the balmy lip crescents on a water glass, & more moons— the polite pile of nail clippings as evidence of your fastidious hygiene rituals before the long flight from me. How many there won't be now.

It wasn't that ours was a lunar relationship, so much as that I liked the moon & tried to locate it everywhere. If I can rouse my new density to elevated ground, I might see the moon through the glassed-over winter skeletons my east coast yore still dreams.

The cold makes me weepy. Creatures must be when things cannot.

I can't stop their rolling back.

wolf

Dear Wolf,

To make a leap of myself, I'd follow your orders, those of animal
lunges and sudden lakes—what we know from our TV screens
and marine shorts. You warmed to the jellyfish's multiple modes
of asexuality. But at the end of the night, it was the drama of male
seahorse birth we remembered best. The wriggling for days to
explode young. Reproduction remained a thing others did, another
form of entertainment we weren't buying.

We've dug our way to the beaches of Lowestoft, where the world is
behind us and before us nothing but emptiness. The trees and silty
waters, steppes and human quiet. Sepia tones, black and white, color:
these affect perception, what I impose. I may not have looked straight
enough. And now, in your germinal best, you can't be specimen, my
pinch-to-tensed-forearm prompt.

Unpacking is left: your skeleton to suit another skin. Undress eyes and
astonish teeth to hasten the canines. The drama of *our* pressing was
an uneven pressure. So this is the passing, pressed a rift.

One day I'll find you by the knobby growth on your spinal column.

Impressed for after,
my cursive L

Dear Leo,

I was on edge when I first fell in with the pups, but they were too young to suspect any difference.

Soon, I think, I will sleep with my ears & nose. A kind of never-forgetting. Never-remembering. The space that must be constantly clear or cleared, ready to be overwhelmed now, a movie-heightened scurry off-camera, the irretrievable arrival of another's scent—what we tried to wash away afterwards.

When control is moot, whose? Will I seek out the ungulate, or the ungulate me, or we each other in compliance with nature's guide to predation? Yes, I will prey upon the old, the young, the sick, the healthy hampered by high snow. But isn't this just compensatory & culling, a eugenicist aid to the enemy? I'd like to believe there's no other way.

If we are both predators, is it as good as saying we're gone & taken up with a new set?

Onward. I'll dream to that.

wolf

Wolf!

I've been shooting from a hot-air balloon. The animals don't even blink. It's this proximity to variegated surface, this spiraling away, this birth on the wind dropping me closer to the ground.

My inventory at seven months: claws, not yet retractable; sensory whiskers; night sprints; the kind of raspy cough I once found attractive in you after so many cigarettes.

One day I'll hide my food in trees.

Is it too late to admit I know nothing about hot-air balloons? I'm only doing my job. Fly-byes across the plains.

Leopard

Your name by shipwreck, less I. Leopardi, of course, my leopard.

I've learned to tear things apart, claw them closer. I drop my teeth inside, wait for clots of wet, nose the acrid, sweet. My miasma triumph. The rending that's always been me.

In leather or linen dinner napkin, designer slippers & winter coats to match manicures. Many cures. Manic ors. Ands. Paratactic pile rugs.

It's me, in essential fur.

& then the reward. Something like: Ada's fascination with an insect's devouring of her mate. Please keep a way.

The fear I vest.

wolf

My Alaskan firecracker,

You reduce wilder. I grow long, would rather be flattened still by you. I look at the shadows of things and conceive a world without specter, a surface where it's high noon all day.

I edge tree-shade all afternoon. You'd toss at such childish logic: what I can't see doesn't exist.

Would you claw my shadow apart? Swallow him whole? If I starved myself, could you locate me by the shadow-tatters stitched across the veld?

Yours,
Leopard

Dear Wolf,

It made me blubber, my obsessive electric crush humming all the
while: "I know that caffeine makes you sad, but just this once won't
you do it for me?"

More me and my inadequacies, you and your inadequacies, and the
impossibility of our intermingling inadequacies. But tell me you knew
that all I wanted was to be unhurried in tall grass with you.

To sit and discover one hundred words for stalks or stars or snow.
For treetop spaces. You. A lexicon of other: sycamore pod-mistletoe,
drowse, -alia.

"It's a place I'd be happy"

Leopard

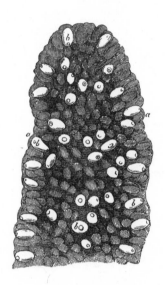

THE MATCHBOOK FRAGMENTS

EXHIB. 6A

low with others

we lend heater-limbs
shed a party to
slouch into a solidity
of down/save
the first pick for alpha

tunnel-moan
then I knew how

EXHIB. 6B

to save the heater
we moan so

-lid slouch low
pick alpha a-
part how

limbs first shed
down other tunnels

EXHIB. 7A

it wasn't
a going to mean
but to sickly

the horizon's informants
& string the sun as tundric

accoutre
-ment with weaves
of our leavings

EXHIB. 7B

the sun it wasn't
but the horizon's
leavings

accoutrement-informants

going as string
with sickly tundric weaves
& to mean

EXHIB. 8A

to proceed
I will clench
the sequence between molars
& trail
pups to sky

the long asked
to lose for a song

look at it
catch in the updrafts
for months
. hide behind snow

months behind
look &
-tween molars

I snow to draft
a sequence for sky

long-up pups
hide song
trail in the clench

EXHIB. 9A

I would sigh
I missed your alpha-

bets/toenail models
but I can't sniff
boot-bottoms or city pebbles

any more than you

EXHIB. 9B

more than alphabet
I miss your model
pebble-sniff

would you sigh

EXHIB. 10A

mark my chalk

fluff too heavy
to waver tongue
cloyed to articulate

I am thick
in my own seams

EXHIB. 10B

seams in
my own cloyed art
tongue thick
to to

CLOSING EXHIB.

swell harlequin:
toast the tourist-cloud
double its usual swoon

& slow our seemly
heads to sleep

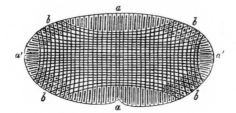

APPENDICES

APPENDIX A:

Photographic Reproduction of *The Matchbook Fragments*

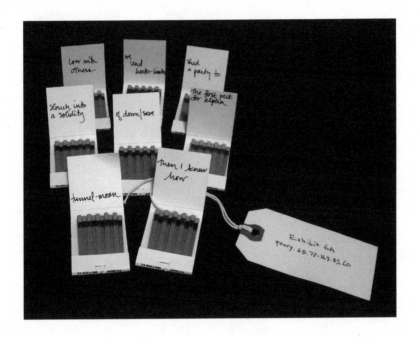

APPENDIX B:
Some Proposals for the Bodyfeel Repository

Exhib. 14
Wolf in outcropping (photograph)

Exhib. 15
Leopard in his leap (photograph)

Exhib. 22
2:00-hot on sorghum shoot (whiff in airtight box)

Exhib. 31
Peary caribou choking on its last breath (audio recording)

Exhib. 36
Musk ox gore-with-fur (licked onto the backside of a postage stamp)

Exhib. 43
Viscosity of musk ox gore-with-fur (testicle-with-earthworm)

APPENDIX C:
A Bodyfeel Lexicon

alpha

n. Zool. One whose matriarchal responsibilities include breeding, regulating body temperature in a new litter, instructing, and hunting.

bind

n. A length of twine or ribbon historically manufactured in two biting intensities.

birdhouse

n. By prior arrangement, a makeshift postbox packed with ice to maintain shape and salt to maintain intention.

bodyfeel

n. Pathol. The exploration by one being of another as wound.

correspondence

n. Claws across the sky.

cuticalia

n. (used with a sing. v.) Tatters like the albino ghosts of eraser scraps.

diorama

n. Wherein one pretends to have therapy every Thursday afternoon, long after one stops going.

father

v. –intr. "When he holds me, heat comes out / of his big arms & I belong to him."

glassy

adj. Genet. Leon Szklar.

leaf

n. A verdant tearing without stakes.

map

n. Whereon pushpins stab points of fraction.

mother

n. Something one moves through. *–v. –intr.* To not turn difficult or wet.

pillowed

adj. Respectful of the impulse to subtle.

prayer

n. A drop in mist. *–v. –intr.* To say one knew a healing wrist, a tongue in one's elbow crook.

pup

n. A fiction, not a lie.

seam

adv. When one must. *–n.* Where two fray.

secret

n. The pocket women's underwear form at the crotch, cotton lining secured at the back end only.

shadow-ghost

n. 1. Something to loosen posture. 2. The noxious weight of what resists unburdening, borne of a fear it might explain. 3. Everything one does to look away. *–v. –intr.* To refract the friendly airs.

theater

n. A distance amenable to disturbance.

torpor

n. A warm cover worn close to the skin, just under sleeves. *–v. –intr.* "You're just going through Halloween, right?"

tourist-cloud

n. A never-deflation, though one might choose to leak it, slowly, and buzz the corner of a room, or the cavern under sheets.

transport

v. –intr. To sting one's skin into a trance.

A PRIMER FOR BOTANICAL AUTOPSY

When wind has unwebbed, sit the visiting bereaved on stumps within the theater.

Open along the glossy-leaved (left) side.

Philodendron the tourists' song down the leaning window's frame.

Record your findings geographically: City plants remnant in oxygen deep in the bones. Diffenbachia, likely 1999. Fossilized herbitage, city-green (yellow with fumes) the meat. A thin layer at the outside, speckled wildflower.

Observe the change in exposed cross-sections.

What of letters, paper-soft & blurred blue? The residue of postage stamp & envelope lick? The wrist bent so often, the hair tucked in mannered agitation? Will we find such crinkled evidence amidst other marrow?

Set the bone-stutters in velvet-lined boxes above index card explanations of origin, destination.

With string, secure the tourists' suspicions that the operators are simulacra of the very bodies they examine.

Shudder as the animals, slowed to tail, push out their sounds.

NOTES

The illustrations are excerpted from Richard Owen's *On the Anatomy of Vertebrates* (London: Longmans, 1868), William Henry Flower's *An Introduction to the Osteology of the Mammalia* (London: Macmillan, 1885), and Sidney F. Harmer and Arthur E. Shipley's *The Cambridge Natural History* (London: Macmillan, 1902).

p. 16: Joseph Beuys; On Kawara

p. 17: *szkło* is Polish for glass

p. 42: *The Rough Guide to Moscow*

p. 66: *Comment naissent les méduses* & *L'hippocampe*, Jean Painlevé; *The Rings of Saturn*, W.G. Sebald

p. 69: *Ada, or Ardor*, Vladimir Nabokov

p. 71: "Shoe-in," The Secret Stars; "One Hundred Words for Snow," Adrian Crowley; "Tugboat," Galaxie 500

p. 95: *Camera Lucida*, Roland Barthes; "Birdie Africa," Lucie Brock-Broido

ACKNOWLEDGMENTS

Excerpts from "Appendix C: A Bodyfeel Lexicon" were published as *cor·re·spon·dence,* a chapbook with Eli Queen, for the dusi/e-chap kollektiv (2007).

"Exhib. 5a" was distributed as *By Prior Arrangement a Makeshift Postbox* in two forms: a fragmented poem-in-matchbooks, in various Athens, Georgia, bars & cafés (November 2006); & a boxed poem-in-matchbooks, via USPS (January 2007). It was also displayed in the Mail Art Exhibition at Niagara Community College Art Gallery (March 18-April 18, 2008).

My sincerest thanks to the editors of the following journals, where some of these poems have appeared, at times in different forms & with different titles: *Apocryphal Text, Columbia Poetry Review, Dusie, Fairy Tale Review, GlitterPony, Gulf Coast, H_ngm_n, Kulture Vulture, LIT, Moonlit, Octopus, P-QUEUE, Shampoo, Spell, Womb.*

I would also like to thank the lovely women at Switchback for their generous support & editorial acuity; Andrew Zawacki, Reginald McKnight, Ed Pavlic & Jordana Rich for their time & invaluable help while I was at the University of Georgia; my workshop allies for eyes & advice; Rae Brune for Barcelona; Jocelyn Glei for fancy pens & resolve; Eli Queen for impromptu lectures, bug-watching with me in Athens, Ole & all the rest.

ABOUT JESSICA BOZEK

Jessica Bozek received an MFA from the
University of Georgia and an MA from the School
of Slavonic and East European Studies in London.
She is the author of *cor·re·spond·ence* (dusi/e-
chap kollektiv), a collaboration with Eli Queen.
She has lived in Russia, England, Spain, and
Costa Rica and currently lives in Cambridge,
Massachusetts. *The Bodyfeel Lexicon* is her
first book.